Oliver's AUsome Week

By Kristian Lee-Morales

Oliver's AUsome Week
By Kristian Lee-Morales
Copyright © 2025 Kristian Lee-Morales
All rights reserved
Published By Kristian Lee-Morales
and B&N press

To my incredible son,

You see the world in a way that is uniquely beautiful, and through your eyes, I have learned to embrace wonder, patience, and strength.

This book is for you—your brilliance, your kindness, and the light you bring to every moment. Never stop being unapologetically you, because you are my greatest inspiration and my most cherished gift.

With all my love,
Mom

Once upon a time, in a colorful little town
there lived a boy named Oliver.
He noticed things that others didn't,
like the way the sun sparkled off the leaves
or how the sound of raindrops
on the roof made a funny rhythm.

But sometimes, Oliver felt a little
different from his friends.

Oliver had something called Asperger's.
That's a word that means his brain worked in a special way.
It helped him think about things deeply and see the world in his own unique way.
But it also meant that sometimes, he didn't understand certain things that other kids did
, like how to talk to them when they looked upset,
Or how to join in their games without feeling nervous.

At school, when the bell rang, everyone would rush to the playground.
Oliver loved the playground, but the noise made him feel dizzy.
The laughing, the shouting, the ringing bells—it was all too much at once.

"I don't know what to do," Oliver thought. "There's too much going on."

So, instead of joining the crowd, Oliver found a quiet spot by the big tree, where he could watch the world from a distance and think about things he loved.

But even though Oliver liked quiet, he also liked people.
He loved to talk about his favorite things, like dinosaurs,
space, and how the stars twinkled at night.
Sometimes, he felt a little unsure of what to say
when his friends wanted to talk about something different.

"Why can't I talk about dinosaurs and stars with everyone?" he wondered.

One day, Oliver's teacher, Mrs. Green, noticed that Oliver was sitting alone again. She walked over and smiled.

"Oliver, would you like to help me with something?" she asked.

Oliver smiled back. He loved to help!

Mrs. Green asked, " Would you like to teach the class about your favorite thing—dinosaurs?"

The next day, Oliver stood in front of the class,
holding a big book about dinosaurs.
He talked about their big teeth, long tails,
and how some of them flew in the sky.
He even told the class which dinosaur might be his best friend if he could meet one!

The kids listened closely, and when Oliver finished, they all clapped.

"Wow, Oliver! You really know a lot about dinosaurs!" said Lily, one of his friends. "I didn't know some of those things!"

From that day on, Oliver realized that it was okay to be different.
He didn't always have to be like everyone else to make friends.
His love for dinosaurs made him special, and that was something worth sharing.

The next day, something amazing happened at recess a few of Oliver's friends came up to him and said, "Can you teach us more about dinosaurs? We want to learn!"

Oliver smiled, and this time, he didn't feel nervous. He was excited. It felt good to share his passion with others.

At the playground, Oliver still liked the quiet, but now, he also played games with his friends sometimes. He didn't always understand every joke or conversation, but he knew that he could be himself—and that was enough.

And that's how Oliver discovered that the world is a wonderful place when we all get to be who we truly are.

At the playground, Oliver still liked the quiet, but now, he also played games with his friends sometimes. He didn't always understand every joke or conversation, but he knew that he could be himself—and that was enough.

And that's how Oliver discovered that the world is a wonderful place when we all get to be who we truly are.

ASPERGER'S SYNDROME, FORMERLY KNOWN AS ASPERGER'S DISORDER, IS A DEVELOPMENTAL DISORDER THAT FALLS UNDER THE UMBRELLA OF AUTISM SPECTRUM DISORDER (ASD). JUST LIKE EVERYONE ELSE, PEOPLE WITH ASPERGER'S CAN HAVE SPECIAL TALENTS, STRONG FEELINGS, AND WONDERFUL THINGS TO SHARE WITH THE WORLD. IF YOU EVER FEEL DIFFERENT, REMEMBER THAT BEING YOURSELF IS WHAT MAKES YOU TRULY AMAZING!

THIS BOOK AIMS TO GENTLY INTRODUCE CHILDREN TO THE CONCEPT OF ASPERGER'S AND OTHER ASD SPECTRUM FORMS, AND HOW EVERYONE IS UNIQUE IN THEIR OWN WAY, FOSTERING EMPATHY AND UNDERSTANDING.

www.ingramcontent.com/pod-product-compliance
Lightning Source LLC
LaVergne TN
LVHW072117060526
838201LV00012B/260